STERNMANIA THE UNOFFICIAL GUIDE TO THE HOWARD STERN SHOW

BY RAY D. O'FAN

A Dell Trade Paperback

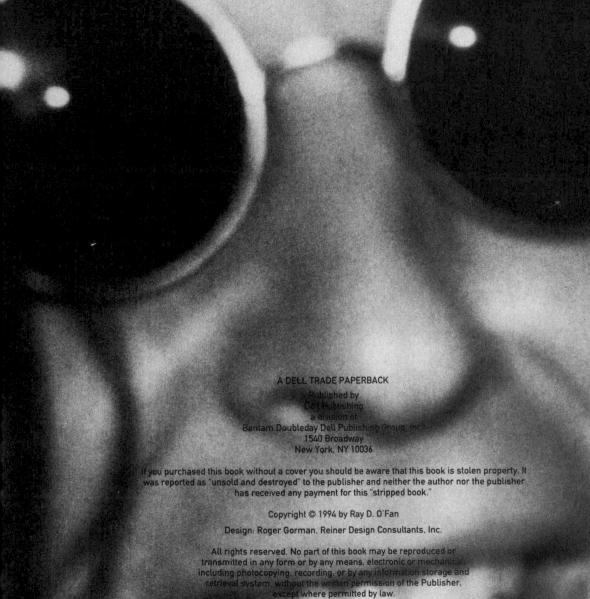

A DELL TRADE PAPERBACK

Published by
Dell Publishing
a division of
Bantam Doubleday Dell Publishing Group, Inc.
1540 Broadway
New York, NY 10036

Copyright © 1994 by Ray D. O'Fan

Design: Roger Gorman, Reiner Design Consultants, Inc.

ISBN: 0-440-50669-7

Printed in the United States of America

Published simultaneously in Canada

February 1994

10 9 8 7 6 5 4 3 2 1

1. Who was Howard singing about in the jig that mentions this person's dead father, brother, sister, one-legged child, and car that doesn't float?

2. Which never happened on the *Howard Stern Show*?

Ⓐ A woman shaved her pubic hair.

Ⓑ Howard ate breakfast for eighteen minutes.

Ⓒ Howard tried to get Ted Nugent's "Wang Dang Sweet Poontang" to be the offical state song of Michigan.

Ⓓ Robin judged a contest for Most Attractive Penis.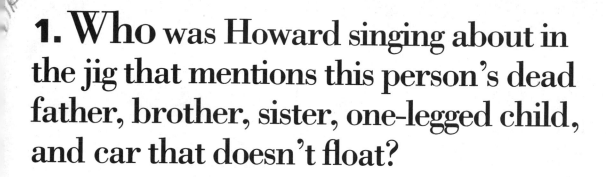

Ⓔ Howard painted women's breasts green for St. Patrick's Day.

Ⓕ Tom Chiusano purchased a state-of-the-art phone system.

3. WHAT ALIAS DID HOWARD USE WHEN HE CALLED TO TALK TO YOKO ONO ON K-ROCK'S "ROCKLINE" (WXRK syndicated show) **?**

4. WHAT SONG DID A TEENAGE HOWARD STERN WRITE AND RECORD WITH HIS BAND?

5. Formerly the Plumbers Union, this band played Jerry Dikowitz's bar mitzvah. Who are they?

6. *Howard Stern has never been a guest on . . .*

(A) *West 57th Street*

(B) *Larry King Live*

(C) *Joan Rivers*

(D) *The Chevy Chase Show*

(E) *Jon Stewart*

(F) *Dick Cavett*

(G) *Geraldo*

(H) *The Larry Sanders Show*

(I) *Nightlife*

(J) *Late Night With David Letterman*

7. What is one of Howard's on-air nicknames for Fred Norris?

8.
What was Product X ?

9. Which of the following experimental operations was not performed by "Kurt Valdheim, Jr"?

Ⓐ **Nipplectemy**

Ⓑ Anus Transplant

Ⓒ # Testicle Tuck

Ⓓ # Road Flare Enema

Ⓔ **Penisectemy**

Ⓕ # Head Transplant

10. Who wrote and recorded "The Pot Song"?

11. Who did the FCC consider "indecent" in transcript in 1987?

Ⓐ **Out of the Closet Stern**

Ⓑ **Sternbo**

Ⓒ **Gay Munsters**

Ⓓ **Ham and Slam**

Ⓔ **Bob and Ray**

Ⓕ **The Satanic Nursery Rhymes**

12. Who recreated the infamous Gary Hart/Donna Rice "Bimini Lap" photo with Howard that appeared in *Star* magazine?

13. What was once **Howard** and **Alison's** pet nickname for each other?

14. Which was never a Howard Stern Show "Dial-a-Date"?

Ⓐ GAY DIAL-A-DATE

Ⓑ HOOKER DIAL-A-DATE

Ⓒ DOMINATRIX DIAL-A-DATE

Ⓓ SMALL PENIS DIAL-A-DATE

Ⓔ FRED NORRIS DIAL-A-DATE

Ⓕ GILBERT GOTTFRIED DIAL-A-DATE

Ⓖ DWARF DIAL-A-DATE

Ⓗ INCONTINENT DIAL-A-DATE

16. On whose answering machine did Howard Stern leave a car-crash sound effect?

17. IN DEEP-VOICE, HOWARD AND ROBIN TRANSFORM INTO TWO GUYS—TWO MANLY MEN THAT BOAST OF WOMEN, BIKES, AND THEIR UNUSUALLY LARGE PENISES AND TESTICLES. WHO ARE THEY?

18.

This department store chain declined to offer its customers Howard Stern's *Private Parts*. It admittedly altered the *New York Times* bestseller list, removing *Private Parts* from it's number-one position and printing a bestseller list without any mention of Stern's book at all.

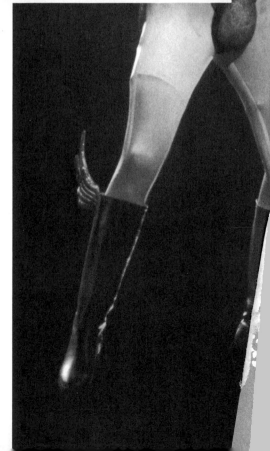

15. Howard Stern has called Boy Gary...

A STINK TOOTH LOSER
B MEATBALL GARY
C LIMBURGER FACE
D KNUCKLEHEAD
E NUMBSKULL
F IMBECILE
G MISTER PENIS
H SCHMUCK
I IDIOT
J RETARD
K DICK
L JERK
M TURD
N LUMOX
O DOPE
P JACKASS
Q SCUM
R FOOL
S SCHMO

T DICKBRAIN
U THE WORST
V MENTAL MIDGET
W DONKEY BOY
X A GOOD PRODUCER
Y A BAD PRODUCER
Z A WACKY PRODUCER
AA A GREAT PRODUCER
BB A TERRIBLE PRODUCER
CC THE YOGI BERRA OF PRODUCERS
DD MUTANT
EE WUSSBAG
FF JELLYFISH
GG HUMAN ANTEATER
HH SQUEAKY BASTARD
II SMELLY BASTARD
JJ BIG DUMB TOOTHY
GUMMED BASTARD
KK ALL OF THE ABOVE

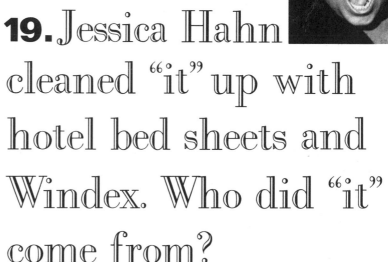

19. Jessica Hahn cleaned "it" up with hotel bed sheets and Windex. Who did "it" come from?

20. He was the only actor with enough balls to introduce Howard as Fartman on the 1992 MTV Music Awards.

21.
Who claimed he would eat a
DEAD DOG'S PENIS
if Howard Stern beat him in the ratings?

22.
On which date in
Howard Stern Show history did
Howard Stern first call Jessica Hahn?

Ⓐ June 3, 1986

Ⓑ June 3, 1987

Ⓒ June 3, 1988

Ⓓ June 3, 1989

23. Who did Howard Stern visit in the hospital after he was stabbed during a march through Brooklyn?

24. What was Howard's reported annual salary when he worked at WCCC in Hartford, Connecticut?

25. Who called Howard a "funny jerk" and "an amusing idiot"?

26. The deadline passed and salad dressing remained on the floor. Howard was furious and began cutting the strings of his piano. He don't like "talking chairs." Who is he?

27. I'm in a club in New Jersey. I just ordered chicken parmigiana. The audience is chanting "Howard! Howard!" Where am I?

MATCHING

28. Howard's first radio job at $96 a week.

29. The station where Robin Quivers first joined Stern.

30. The station where Fred Norris first joined Stern.

31. The station where Gary Dell'Abate first joined Stern.

32. The station where Jackie Martling first joined Stern.

33. The station where Stuttering John Melendez first joined Stern

Ⓐ WWDC   **Ⓒ** WYSP   **Ⓔ** WRNW   **Ⓖ** WWWW

Ⓑ WNBC   **Ⓓ** WCCC   **Ⓕ** WXRK

34. WHAT MEDICAL PROBLEM REAR-ENDED HOWARD STERN?

35. How many times were the words "man" and "dude" used during the infamous "Howard Stern-Sam Kinison Fight" phone call?

Ⓐ 0 TO 24 TIMES

Ⓑ 25 TO 49 TIMES

Ⓒ 50 TO 74 TIMES

Ⓓ 75 TO 99 TIMES

Ⓔ 100 TO 124 TIMES

Ⓕ OVER 125 TIMES

36. Who sang "Leader of the Pack" with Howard in a Mexican cantina in London?

37. What camp did Howard Stern attend in his younger years?

- Ⓐ Camp Beth-El
- Ⓑ Camp Bené
- Ⓒ Camp Trimmabush
- Ⓓ Camp Wel-Met
- Ⓔ Camp Pouch
- Ⓕ Joy Camp

38. Howard tied him up on *Comedy Tonight* back in 1985 and stuffed a red **S&M** ball into his mouth.

39. In which box did Howard Stern sit when he was a guest on *Hollywood Squares*?

1	2	3
4	5	6
7	8	9

40.
Who did Howard hug and pet affectionately when he made his raucous appearance on the *Tonight Show* with Jay Leno?

41. On which late-night television show did Howard Stern's mother make a **SURPRISE** guest appearance?

42. Howard and Fred once performed **"The Guidelines Are A-Changin"** on MTV's Headbangers Ball. Who was that night's host?

43. In 1987 Howard did five summer television pilots that never aired. Which network were these for?

44. ON WHOSE SHOW DID HOWARD MAKE HIS FIRST WASHINGTON, D. C., TELEVISION APPEARANCE... IN BLACKFACE?

Ⓐ Judd Rose
Ⓑ Charlie Rose
Ⓒ Petey Green
Ⓓ Maury Povich
Ⓔ Larry King
Ⓕ Uncle Floyd

45.
When Fred plays a cascade of circus sounds, belly laughs, hoots 'n hollers, who's it time for Howard to plug?

46. On the *Stern Show*'s first trip to Philadelphia, what costume did Howard wear when he triumphantly took the stage?

47. WHO WAS ROBIN DRESSED AS?

48. What coveted award is given annually by the *Howard Stern Show?*

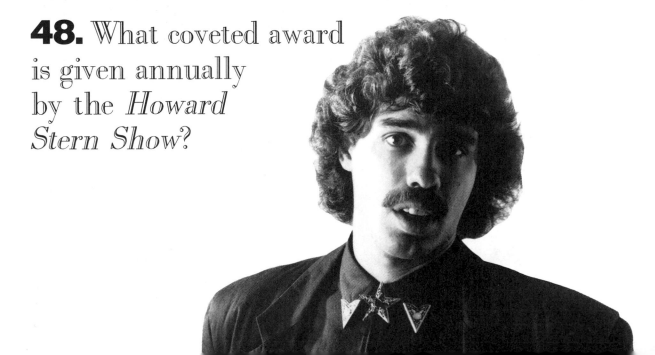

TRUE OR FALSE

49. The *Howard Stern Show* begins at 6 a.m. and ends at 10 a.m.

50. Howard's parents meditate.

51. Fred's girlfriend is named Alison.

52. Robin was a nurse in the navy.

53. Mary married Gary.

54. In a song, Stuttering John once called Robin a porch monkey.

55. Jackie the Jokeman once stuck his finger up Steve O's butt.

56. Fred Norris was born in Spring Hill, Florida.

57. Robin has undergone breast enlargement surgery.

58. HOWARD'S FAMILY NICKNAME IS HOWCHIE.

59. *Who won Howard Stern's 1986 Felt Forum New Year's Eve Beauty Pageant? He still has a penis and three nipples.*

60.
WHO LICKED ROBIN QUIVERS' FEET AND, BECAUSE HE LOST TO HER IN A TENNIS MATCH, WAS NEVER SUPPOSED TO BOTHER HER AGAIN.

61. Who coined the phrase *"mama lucien"* and helped introduce 'Gina Man to the show?

62. Who was told to put her clothes back on at an annual Christmas show? She inspired the phrase

"Tom Fruise."

63. HE USED TO BE A FREQUENT CALLER AT WNBC AND WXRK... HOWARD DEDICATES HIS "CRUCIFIED BY THE FCC" BOX SET TO THIS LEGENDARY CALLER. HE'S DEAD... GOOD NIGHT FUNNYMAN. WHO IS HE?

64.
She sucked Howard's toes
and claims to be one of the first guests to spank him in the studio.

65. Who were the three "afflicted" listeners that starred in the *Howard Stern Show* production of "*A C...C...Christmas C...C...Carol*"?

66. This wild street musician once broke into

Yoko Ono's

apartment. Howard had him on as a guest almost immediately.

67. Who drags a foot?

68. WHO PLAYS KEYBOARD WITH HER TONGUE AND PERFORMED "THE STAR-SPANGLED BANNER" TO A PACKED NASSAU COLISEUM AT STERN'S "U.S. OPEN SORES"?

69. Which of the following never has been a Howard Stern "double entendre" term for penis?

Ⓐ Trouser Trout

Ⓑ Wahdoobee

Ⓒ Meat Baton

Ⓓ One-Eyed Weasel

Ⓔ Boobshenga

Ⓕ Dinktadanker

Ⓖ Johnson

Ⓗ Weenie Schmeister

70. Who does Howard Stern credit with bringing him to New York?

Ⓐ RICHARD JOHNSON

Ⓑ JERRY NACHMAN

Ⓒ EDIE MCCLURG

Ⓓ DON IMUS

Ⓔ BOB GUCCIONE, JR.

Ⓕ BOB MORTON

71. Howard grew up in this suburb on Long Island.

72. When Howard finally moved, he went to <u>this town</u>, finished high school, then went on to Boston University, where he graduated magna cum laude in 1976.

73.

WHEN THIS PERSON EATS, HOWARD SAYS HE STORES HIS FOOD IN A POUCH.

74. WHOSE BASEMENT GOT FLOODED DURING THE 1993 NOREASTER?

75. When you hear the sound effect of a golf swing, who has entered the room?

76. What was the name of Howard Stern's Boston University radio show?

77. What bit did Howard broadcast just

BEFORE HE GOT FIRED?

78. Who fired him, on the air, on his first show?

79. This Zookeeper finally left Philly morning radio...after a Stern mock funeral...after a separation from his wife...after his ratings nearly disappeared.

80. He doesn't call Howard a Shock Jock...he likes to call him a

"SCHLOCK JOCK." Who is he?

81. Who called Sam Kinison "Jabba the Hut" on the show?

Ⓐ Bobcat Goldthwait   Ⓓ Andrew Dice Clay

Ⓑ Richard Lewis   Ⓔ Robin Quivers

Ⓒ Judy Tenuta   Ⓕ Malika Kinison

82. Who sang "Why Isn't Howard Stern on TV"?

83. Although Howard refused to go to see *The Prince of Tides* with him, Robin did accompany him to see the Broadway bomb *Legs Diamond*.

84. This band won a song parody contest and went on to become known as Howard Stern's band. They are recording artists...

85. Who was **"Pig Virus"** at WNBC?

Ⓐ Dale Parsons

Ⓑ John Hayes

Ⓒ Bob Sherman

Ⓓ Kevin Metheny

Ⓔ Randy Bongarten

Ⓕ Bob Mountie

Family Roll Call

What are the first names of the following Stern family members?

86. Howard's mother?

87. Howard's father?

88. Howard's mother-in-law?

89. Howard's father-in-law?

90. Howard's sister?

91. Howard's first daughter?

92. Howard's second daughter?

93. Howard's third daughter?

94. Howard's family cat?

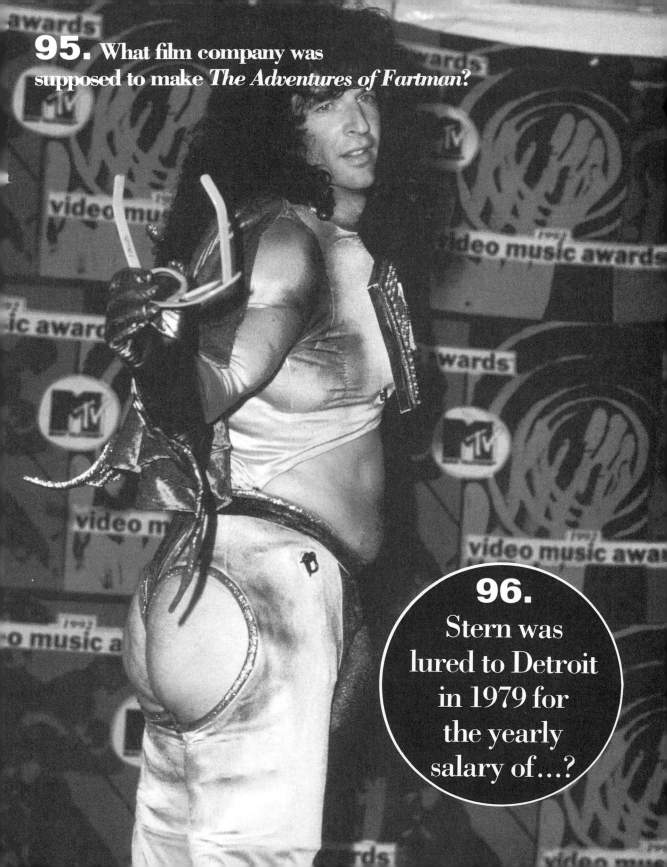

95. What film company was supposed to make *The Adventures of Fartman?*

96. Stern was lured to Detroit in 1979 for the yearly salary of...?

97. Howard left

WWWW

because overnight the station changed to what format?

98. When Howard was just a kid, he visited his father's recording studio, and, although interrupted, sang this childhood song solo.

99. What two food items—

one protein, one carbohydrate—

were/are the regimented staple of Howard's diet?

100. What promotional item was given to each customer who got a full tank of a Northville gas? It sported a caricatured self-portrait and autograph of Howard Stern.

101. Although short lived, what did D.I.R. Broadcasting/Lorimar productions hire Howard and company to do?

102. *Who called Howard a* "Slimeburger to the max" *on his own late-night television show?*

103. Who said that Howard had the "brain of an egg timer."

104. Of the following, who was not a member "**POND SCUM**

Ⓐ T. Bone   Ⓑ Stevie Ray Vaughan

Ⓒ Joe Franco   Ⓓ Leslie West

105. Where was Howard's 1987 Anti-Censorship Freedom rally held?

106. What did an overzealous **Grandpa Al Lewis** of the *Munsters* yell out to a cheering audience...live...on the air...at the freedom rally?

of Howard Stern's Birthday show band

COMBO''?

Ⓔ Alan St. John   **Ⓕ** Adam Tisi   **Ⓖ** Dee Snider

107. Of the following, who did not make an appearance at the freedom rally?

A Leslie West

B Dee Snider

C Lisa Sliwa

D Phoebe Snow

E Tom Chiusano

F Susan Berkley

108. In the Stern bit "Return to Mayberry R.F.D.: 25 Years Later", who was the biggest cocaine dealer in town?

109.

At an annual *Howard Stern Show* Christmas Party broadcast, who was hypnotized to feel sexually aroused each time Howard rubbed his own ear?

110. *When she finally calmed down, she was hypnotized to speak <u>this</u> foreign language.*

111. On what magazine cover did a drawing of Howard appear? He was pictured naked, arms tied behind his back, a microphone stuffed into his mouth, and with a black woman shoving a watermelon up his butt.

112. When Howard first called **Jessica Hahn,** who was his in-studio guest?

Ⓐ Penn Jillette Ⓑ Judy Tenuta Ⓒ Richard Belzer
Ⓓ Emo Phillips Ⓔ Gilbert Gottfried Ⓕ Ted the Janitor

What vintage Stern Show bits are these?

113. CRANTES

114. KALBC OEYRPJAD

115. YEYMRTS UTGES

116. AEERVB RABKES

117. OIRDEP OPLO

118. YEYSRMT ZWIH

119. OOBTAHMR LCSYOMPI

120. CREPGNNYA RLPOAT

121. TNTCAOC LISVE

122. ROTBESN

123. Which general manager of Howard's was once treated for Rocky Mountain spotted fever?

Ⓐ Randy Bongarten

Ⓑ John Hayes

Ⓒ Dom Fioravanti

Ⓓ Goff Lebhar

Ⓔ Steve Chiconas

Ⓕ Tom Chiusano

127. Howard's mother was told by a doctor after his birth that he looked as happy as a what?

128. What was Howard's father's favorite come-home-from-work, time-to-relax cocktail?

They talked about and planned this event for weeks. All the guys on the show would do a striptease on stage at the 1986 New Year's Eve Show at Madison Square Garden.
WHAT OUTFIT DID EACH SEXY MALE STRIPPER WEAR WHEN THEY STARTED TO...TAKE IT OFF?

129. Gary was...   **131.** Fred was...

130. Jackie was...   **132.** Howard was...

124. When Howard, Robin, and Fred left WWDC, which one of them was not a part of the early WNBC team?

125. She was "the cleaning lady" at WNBC.

126. Which bit got Howard his first suspension while broadcasting at WNBC?

Ⓐ God Weather
Ⓑ I Shred Lucy
Ⓒ Pernicious Anemia
Ⓓ Tennis without Balls
Ⓔ Virgin Mary Kong
Ⓕ Beastiality Dial-a-Date

133. If you mail in a nude photo of yourself to Howard's WXRK office, where might it wind up?

Howard returned to Philadelphia in June of 1992 and triumphantly claimed complete victory over the "Zookeeper." With thousands of cheering fans filling the streets, Howard and Robin greeted their loyal listeners in full regalia.

134. What was Howard dressed as?

135. Who was Robin dressed as?

136. What was the name Howard dubbed this event?

137. This song won the listener song parody contest and was sung to the theme of 2001: A Space Odyssey.

138. Howard had an on-air shoving match with <u>this</u> WNBC general manager.

139. Howard calls him "The Incubus." Who is he?

Ⓐ John Hayes   Ⓓ Mark Chernoff

Ⓑ Randy Bongarten   Ⓔ Dom Fioravanti

Ⓒ Tom Chiusano   Ⓕ Andy Bloom

140. Howard was suspended a second time at WNBC for this bit.

Ⓐ Pregnancy Patrol

Ⓑ Sexual Innuendo Wednesday

Ⓒ Hill Street Jews

Ⓓ Das Love Boot

Ⓔ Lance the Hairdresser

Ⓕ Bathroom Olympics

When Howard made his parody of *Bill and Ted's Excellent Adventure* he used the talents of these two performers:

141. She was once hired for a week as the prize and weather girl.

142. He was a janitor. He wanted to "play road" with Robin.

143. Which Howard Stern character recited his manly poem …"Kill Kill Kill…the hippies"?

144. From which bit came the line "I got a woody that won't quit."
A The Siobhanny Mooners
B Rocky and Bullwinkle
C Return to Mayberry
D Gay Munsters
E Freddy Krueger vs. Fartman

145. "La Da Dee"… Howard is dialing….whose answering machine once played "Maybe I'll call you, maybe I won't"?

146. Given…**WXRK = 92.3.** Add **WXRK, WYSP,** and **WJFK.** Rounded off, what is the total?

147. He didn't trust repentent ex-preacher Sam Kinison after the "Bon Jovi" incident, so Sam accused him of sucking on gas fumes. Who is Howard's faithful limo driver?

148. Howard Stern's cousin is a member of which band?

Ⓐ **Blue Oyster Cult**

Ⓑ **Blue Cheer**

Ⓒ **Psychedelic Lollipops**

Ⓓ **Grand Funk Railroad**

Ⓔ **Iron Butterfly**

Ⓕ **Rockslide**

149. On which magazine cover did Howard Stern appear wearing a full length leather jacket?

Ⓐ *Penthouse* Ⓓ *GQ*
Ⓑ *Esquire* Ⓔ *Rolling Stone*
Ⓒ *Time* Ⓕ *Whole Life*

150. At WNBC who went to bat for Howard and spent ten minutes yelling at his general manager Dom Fioravanti?

151. When Howard appeared on David Brenner's late-night television show Nightlife, he gave Brenner's then girlfriend four gifts. Name one.

152. What group backed Stern when he first sang the "Len Bias Blues"?

Ⓐ **Pig Vomit**

Ⓑ **Stray Cats**
Ⓒ **The Fabulous Thunderbirds**
Ⓓ **Josie Sang**
Ⓔ **The Washington Squares**

Below is a diagram of WXRK's studio, where Howard broadcasts his show each and every weekday morning at six. Where do Jackie, Fred, Robin, and Howard sit?

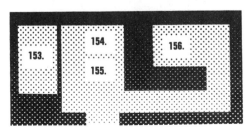

157.
This syndicated newspaper comic strip spent a week lampooning Howard Stern in 1993.

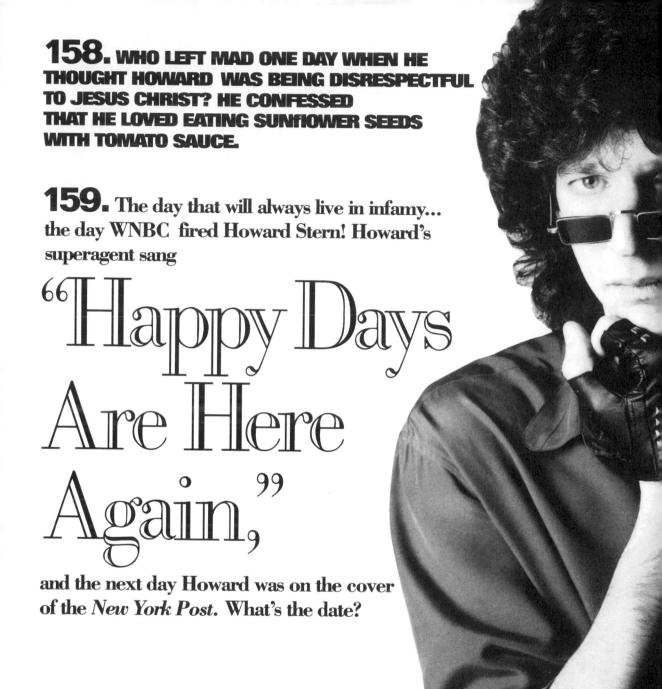

158. WHO LEFT MAD ONE DAY WHEN HE THOUGHT HOWARD WAS BEING DISRESPECTFUL TO JESUS CHRIST? HE CONFESSED THAT HE LOVED EATING SUNFLOWER SEEDS WITH TOMATO SAUCE.

159. The day that will always live in infamy... the day WNBC fired Howard Stern! Howard's superagent sang "Happy Days Are Here Again," and the next day Howard was on the cover of the *New York Post*. What's the date?

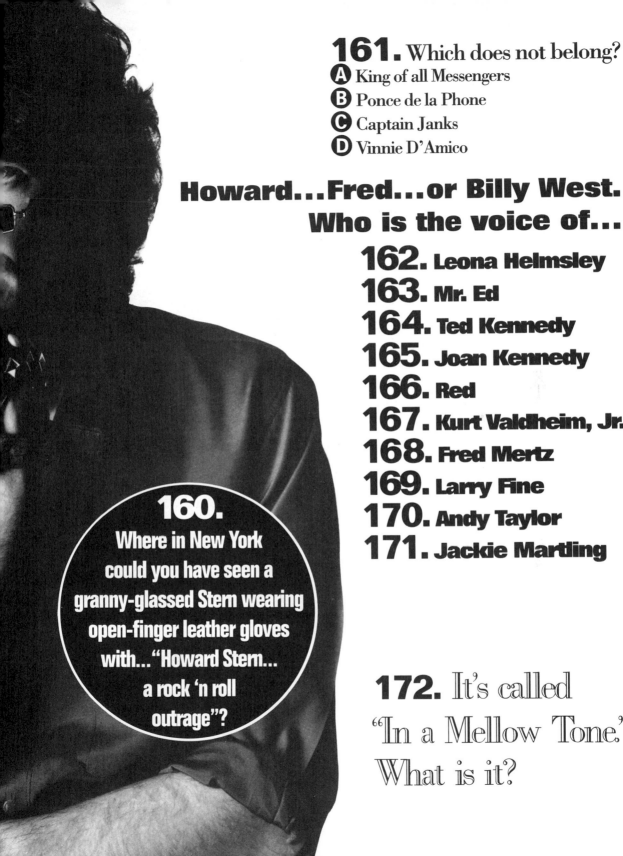

161. Which does not belong?

Ⓐ King of all Messengers
Ⓑ Ponce de la Phone
Ⓒ Captain Janks
Ⓓ Vinnie D'Amico

Howard...Fred...or Billy West. Who is the voice of...

162. Leona Helmsley

163. Mr. Ed

164. Ted Kennedy

165. Joan Kennedy

166. Red

167. Kurt Valdheim, Jr.

168. Fred Mertz

169. Larry Fine

170. Andy Taylor

171. Jackie Martling

160. Where in New York could you have seen a granny-glassed Stern wearing open-finger leather gloves with... "Howard Stern... a rock 'n roll outrage"?

172. It's called "In a Mellow Tone." What is it?

173. Grammy's biggest fight scenario! After calling out her name numerous times, this comedienne's escort pushed a megaphone into Howard's face and started a minibrawl!

174. In the ensuing tussle, who took a punch for his boss?

175. Howard's best line in Spanish. Translate... "mis avios de pescar en la cocina."

176. Howard Stern held the number-one spot on the *New York Times* bestseller list for four straight weeks in the fall of 1993. His book, *Private Parts*, was the fastest-selling book in Simon and Schuster's 75-year history. Who came up with the title right on the show?

177. Who replaced Howard on WNBC after he was fired?

Ⓐ Alan Colmes
Ⓑ Al Rosenberg
Ⓒ Soupy Sales
Ⓓ Joey Reynolds
Ⓔ Mark the Shark
Ⓕ Jay Thomas

178. What did Governor-elect **Christine Todd Whitman** of New Jersey **promise Howard** she would do if she won the 1993 Gubernatorial election?

179. *She* questions Howard's "hot-with-cold-food" eating habits and has been known to pat his head. *He* leaves newspapers on the couch and asks endless celebrity questions. Who are they? *Last name only*!

180. What state were they from when Howard first met them?

Which Intern?

181. Picked up and dropped off a homeless man in a New York subway.

182. Has sum sbelling prablums.

183. "Rockslide."

184. Annoyed Dr. Ruth by telling her that he had anal sex with his roommate.

185. Was hypnotized to be jealous and possessive of Howard...wrote poems.

186. Auditioned as an extra in a Spike Lee movie.

Ⓐ "Dead Dave"
Ⓑ Mike Gange
Ⓒ Jackie The Intern
Ⓓ Stuttering John Melendez
Ⓔ Steve Grillo
Ⓕ Mitch The Intern

187. Howard and Robin tormented her daily. She was shadow traffic reporter Susan "Berserkowitz." What's her real name?

188. When **Judy Tenuta** ran off the show crying, who was not present?

Ⓐ Jack Riley   Ⓓ Chuck McCann
Ⓑ Penn Jillette   Ⓔ Pat McCormick
Ⓒ Sam Kinison   Ⓕ Pat Cooper

189. He once headed the "National Conference for Decency" and reported Stern to the FCC for broadcasting patently offensive material in 1986.

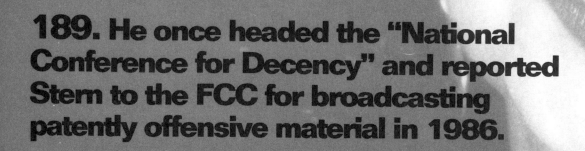

190. In 1990 the FCC fined three stations $2,000 each for airing Stern's Christmas show of 1988. Which three stations were fined?

191.
This *Stern Show* saboteur, armed with telephone, tape recorder and harmonizer, began his brand of guerrilla phony phone calls as a captain in the thirty-sixth field artillery in the Federal Republic of Germany.

192. He ends every phone appearance with

"Stay well, I love you"

and won the 1993 F Emmy for Best Phony Phone Call.

193. *Who did Howard and Fred strike up a conversation with in a bathroom while he was sitting on the bowl?*

194. Who was Howard's weatherman in Washington, D. C.?

195. Who did leather weather in Detroit?

196. Who boxed Geraldo Rivera and won a three-round decision?

197. Howard called him to mediate a comedy feud…

but a slurred Sam Kinison threatened to kick his ass.

198. Who jumped into Jessica Hahn's bathtub and immediately turned the water black?

199. What band shared the stage with Fartman on the 1992 MTV Music Awards?

200. This beehived columnist once wrote that Howard was a "six foot five radio person with the seven foot three mouth." She says Howard likes to make "Cindyburgers" out of her.

201. When Sam Kinison promised to bring Jon Bon Jovi to the station to finally make peace with Howard, who was Stern's in-studio guest?

202. In which magazine did Howard appear in 1984 dressed as a devil with a bad mustache?

(A) *The Sun*
(B) *Steppin' Out*
(C) *Playboy*
(D) *People*
(E) *US*
(F) *Life*

203. Howard read about it in a local newspaper. Who was issued a summons for turnstile jumping?

204. He called NBC's *Today* show and asked Ross Perot "Have you ever had the desire to mind meld with Howard Stern's penis?" Who'd he call as?

205. She was the Philly Zookeeper's ex-wife...did Dial-a-Date with Howard and then— call it fate—dated **Captain Janks.**

206. She worked with Howard in Detroit...they've worked back-to-back shifts at WXRK...and she once described Stern's studio as "Dante's Inferno."

A Lisa Sliwa

B Roz Frank

C Alison Steele

D The "Madame"

E Melissa Gilbert

F Meg Griffen

207. What movie did a teenage Howard Stern see with his father?

They were both a little embarrassed.

208. Howard's boyhood friend. He told Howard to play the field, but he got all the girls. Now he's a doctor.

209. On Howard's first real date with Alison, what movie did they see?

210. WHO CLAIMS TO HAVE CHONDROMALACIA OF THE KNEE?

211. Where was Howard working when he won the *Billboard* award for best AOR disc jockey?

212 When Howard borrowed the family car for precollege dates, what make car was his date treated to?

Ⓐ **1970 Valiant**

Ⓑ **Mercury Montego**

Ⓒ Chevy Malibu

Ⓓ **Ford Suburban Wagon**

Ⓔ **Dodge Dart**

Ⓕ **Rambler**

213. Who attended the University of Michigan for Engineering?

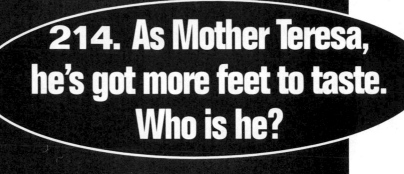

214. As Mother Teresa, he's got more feet to taste. Who is he?

215. What word did Stuttering John use in an interview with Walter Cronkite that made him question John about its journalistic use?

216. HOWARD DEFEATED THIS DJ TEAM FROM LOS ANGELES IN LESS THAN A YEAR AND CEREMONIOUSLY, IN FRONT OF THOUSANDS OF CHEERING FANS, CUT OFF THEIR HEADS!

217. THAT'S WHY ROBIN WAS DRESSED AS WHO?

218. From Melrose Avenue in Los Angeles to Madison Avenue in New York he can be heard muttering "Baba Booey" while displaying a plethora of homemade signs. Who is he?

219. When a young Howard went to sleep-away camp as a maturing teenage **geek**, he wore sunglasses to look cool. What was he nicknamed?

220. When Stern left for New York this DJ was hired by WWDC. Nowadays his commercial spots during Howard's show seem to always have audio problems. Who is he?

221. Recently, he made his acting debut in an off-off-Broadway play. Name him.

222. Where did the infamous "Howard Stern/Scott Muni" confrontation take place in London?

223. What do **Mary Keeley, Anne Stommel,** and **Al Wescot** all have in common?

224. When Alison, Emily, and Debra visited the studio to meet the Olsen twins, what song did Emily perform?

225. To whom did Howard offer a vacation trip to Montego Bay in Jamaica?

Ⓐ Donna Rice

Ⓑ Lynn Armandt

Ⓒ Jessica Hahn

Ⓓ Fawn Hall

Ⓔ Shelly the Typist

Ⓕ Becky the Mental Patient

226. Howard Stern was **born in 1954.** When is his birthday?

227. Howard took Abbie Hoffman down there once. And on a trip with Dee Snider and DJ Bob Wah, a rattlesnake bit Howard's genitals. The door creaks, the stairs are steep, and the sound of constant dripping fills this mythical radio place. What is it?

228. What is the name of Howard's only album, recorded while in Washington, D.C.? It came with a poster.

229. The week he was fired from WNBC Howard was sporting crutches. Which foot was injured?

230. What mask was Howard wearing when he went **"trick-or-treating"** in Bayside, Queens (New York), and managed to get treated to a bedroom massage?

A Bart Simpson   **D** Marge Simpson

B Ronald Reagan   **E** Barbie

C Batman   **F** Fred Flintstone

231. What Dick Clark game show was Robin Quivers a guest on?

232. He called in sort of regularly with a weekly football report but Howard always managed to talk about his white wife. Who is he?

233. When Milton Berle first appeared on the show, Howard lined up a few choice callers. What was every single question about?

234. What's Howard's nickname for *Entertainment Tonight* host John Tesh?

235. When Janis Ian performed her hit "At Seventeen" on the show, who accompanied her on lead guitar?

236. *When Howard pulls the "shoe trick," what do the guys get to see?*

237. BEFORE HE WAS BABA BOOEY, HE WAS SIMPLY BOY GARY, AND WHEN GARY BOUNCED INTO THE STUDIO, FRED WAS SURE TO PLAY THIS SONG. WHAT IS IT?

238. On whose answering machine was the following: "If you're anybody but Howard Stern please leave your message after you hear the warbling sound . . . here it comes"?

A Jerry Seinfeld **D** Dick Cavett

B Steve Rossi **E** Pat Cooper

C Al Rosenberg **F** Steve "Maddog" Chiconas

239.

Although he would settle for the remains of
"skunk girl," "sheep boy," or "chicken girl,"
Howard really wanted to put in a bid for whose remains?

240. On the box cover of *"Crucified by the FCC,"* Howard's face is superimposed over the face of Jesus. Who did the original painting?

A Pablo Pickcotton   **D** Vincent Van Washington

B El Greco   **E** Peter Max

C Raphael   **F** Giotto

241. Who is Howard's **"superagent"**?

242. Dee Snider and company, and Howard Stern and company, almost came to blows and fisticuffs with which band in London?

A Alan Parsons Project

B Sigue Sigue Sputnik

C The Bee Gees

D The Plumbers Union

E The Clash

243. As a guest cohost on New York's Easter Seals Telethon, Howard once said that the only thing worse than sitting "in this wheelchair are these _____ I rented from this store in Queens."

244. To which Academy Award-winning actress did Boy Gary ask "Do you know Susan Berkley?"

245. She does a mean Cher impersonation, and once brought a monkey doll named Linus into the studio. She said it was her son. Her last name is LaRosa. Who is she?

246. Where did Howard and Alison go on their honeymoon?

Ⓐ Florida   Ⓒ Mexico   Ⓔ Hawaii

Ⓑ Aruba   Ⓓ Boston   Ⓕ France

247. He sang a medley of show tunes for the big L.A. rally and is married to Martha Raye. "Dice" called him a parasite. Who is he?

248. **As a child,** what did Howard bury in his parents' backyard?

What are/were Howard's nicknames for the following:

249. Jon Bon Jovi ... Jon Bon _____

250. David Lee Roth ... David _____ Roth

251. John Cougar Mellencamp ... John Cougar _____

252. Hempstead, Long Island ... Hempstead, _____

253. Kathie Lee Gifford ... Kathie _____ Gifford

254. Howard Stern's book party for his number-one bestseller *Private Parts* was held at the Harley Davidson Cafe in New York. Writers, musicians, comedians, and show-biz celebrities of all types paraded in to pay homage to the "King of All Media." Who wasn't there?

Sally Kirkland	Pat Cooper	Joey Buttafuoco
Mr. T.	Clarence Clemens	Joey Ramone
Joan Rivers	Marvin Kitman	David Lee Roth
Ed Koch	Dee Snider	Grandpa Al Lewis
Senator Al D'Amato	Jessica Hahn	Lloyd Lindsay Young
Geraldo Rivera	Gilbert Gottfried	Wendy "The Snapple Lady"
Noel Redding	Dominic Barbara	

255. Who accidentally **threw urine** in their mother's face?

256. The "You Dick" cart made guest Richard Simmons go crazy. Who's voice yells "you dick" (not to be confused with the "You Stupid Dick" jingle)?

257. Peter Noone of Herman's Hermits sang this irreverent Stern parody about a former first lady. What is the name of the song?

258. Medical waste washed ashore on the beaches of Long Island a few years ago, so Howard "deep voiced" this song. What is it?

259. When Kay Gardella reviewed Stern's Pay-Per-View special ... and hadn't seen it yet ... Fred got busy, and recorded this.

260. When Sammy Davis, Jr. died, a raspy-voiced Jackie Martling sang this version of **"The Candy Man."**

261. Which televison show theme did Howard play backwards, listening for hidden satanic messages?

262. Who once said, "Ratings Schmatings! I don't care."?

263. In what film did Howard Stern make a cameo appearance?

264. In this film Howard played a news reporter for Channel 14 news. Who was he?

265. "What would it be like without radio?" James Earl Jones announced this 30-second moment of silence to illustrate the importance of radio in contemporary society. Howard, of course, had a different idea. As the moment approached, a hushed Stern crew giggled their way past the first few seconds ... then ... what sound effect shattered the silence?

A "You Dick!"

B "Hello Frisco"

C A car crash

D Farting sounds

E "Shut up. Sit Down."

F The Hindenberg disaster cart

266. Joan Rivers played matchmaker once when Robin appeared as a guest on her daytime talk show. Which soap opera star did Joan hook Robin up with?

Howard, over the phone, hooked up these two music legends to play

"Theme from an Imaginary Western":

267. He played transatlantic lead guitar from the United States.

268. This legendary bass player sat with Stern in London, sang, and played keyboards.

269. WHEN THE BEE GEES STOPPED BY, THEY SANG A POTPOURRI OF THEIR FINEST SONGS. WHICH GIBB, HOWEVER, REVEALED THAT HE WAS MARRIED TO A LESBIAN?

Almost all the guys stripped down to their underwear to have Robin evaluate their bodies.

270. Who did Robin give a **"10"** to?

271. Who did Robin give an **"8.5"** to?

272. To whom did she give an **"8"**?

273. Who wouldn't take off his clothes?

274. Before he worked in radio in Westchester, New York, what advertising agency did Howard briefly work for?

275. Before Robin hooked up with Howard, she worked in a Baltimore, Maryland, radio station. What was her job?

276. Who is King of all Faxes?

277. Howard and Robin said Gary wore this T-shirt three times in one week. Jackie laughed aloud that it was definitely in heavy rotation. Gary is pictured wearing it in Stern's *Private Parts*. What cartoon character is on the shirt?

278. On what magazine cover was Howard pictured near a sidebar that read "Howard Stern has a very small penis"?

279. Who called Gary's home answering machine looking to talk to Stern but hung-up after uttering a mumbled "Welcome to my nightmare"?

280. Although it was the number one requested song on K-Rock for a week or so, Howard never released it as a single, but performed it live on New Year's eve in 1986. What is the name of the song?

281. Only days
BEFORE SENTENCING, HE ATTENDED HOWARD'S BOOK PARTY WITH HIS WIFE AND ATTORNEY.

282. In what year did Howard Stern first debut on WNBC, New York?

(A) 1981 **(B)** 1982 **(C)** 1983 **(D)** 1984

283.
Spell Gary's last name.

284. On who's late-night show did Howard blame Fox for the suicide death of Joan Rivers's husband, the late Edgar Rosenberg?

285. In what magazine was Howard and Robin featured as **"Howard Stoned and Bobin"** visiting a fat farm?

286. This *Eight is Enough* star revealed to Howard that she was kidnapped for 2 months in South Korea. Who is she?

287. His daughter said he was never there, his son interned for *Geraldo*, even his mother got in on the original phone-fight conversation. He's shot out of a cannon. Who is he?

288. This former Manhattan US attorney backed the DEA's decision to open a preliminary drug investigation of Stern in 1988. Who is he?

289. Who has a **berry** on his face?

290. In what branch of the armed services did Robin serve?
Ⓐ Army Ⓑ Navy Ⓒ Air Force Ⓓ Marines

291. In his college days Howard asked Alison to be in his student film. What was the subject of this documentary?

292. On what date did the *New York Times* first list Howard Stern's *Private Parts* as it's number-one bestseller?

Ⓐ October 10 Ⓑ October 17 Ⓒ October 24 Ⓓ October 31

293. WHEN HOWARD FIRST CALLED CHEVY CHASE AT HOME, WHO WAS HIS GUEST?

294. When Howard asked Abbie Hoffman if he was ever attracted to another man, who did Abbie mention?

295. With the help of Howard Stern's persistant prodding, who revealed on the *Joan Rivers Show* that she once walked in on David Bowie and Mick Jagger together ... in bed ... naked!

On the following pages you will find an extensive list of celebrities. Of these celebrities, which five were never guests (either in-studio or on the phone) on the Howard Stern Show?

296. _____

297. _____

298. _____

299. _____

300. _____

Abbie Hoffman
Axl Rose
Alec Baldwin
Albert Brooks
Al Roker
Anson Williams
Alison Steele
Arnold Schwarzenegger
Alice Cooper
Andrew Dice Clay
Al Sharpton
Al Michael

Bob Hope
Bobcat Goldthwait
Beverly D'Angelo
Bill Cosby
Buddy Hackett
Branford Marsalis
Brian Wilson
Bryan Adams
Bonnie Raitt
Belinda Carlisle
Bob Geldof
Bill Beutel
Bob Denver
Barbara Eden
Bill Boggs
Billy Preston
Bob Saget
Barry Nolan
Bobby Vinton
Bob Eubanks
Britt Ekland
Boy George
Bob Wahl
Bob Nelson

Chris Robinson
Cheech Marin

Chuck McCann
Chip Z'Nuff
Charles Barkley
Carol Leifer
Chuck Norris
Corey Feldman
Curtis Sliwa
Corbin Bernsen
Cyndi Lauper
Carly Simon
Clarence Clemens
Chevy Chase
Corey Haim
Carol Alt

Dick Butkus
Danny Bonaduce
Dana Carvey
Duff
Deborah Harry
Dee Snider
Dom DeLuise
Dick Cavett
Dick York
Dick Clark
David Faustino
David Brenner
David Lee Roth
Dennis Hopper
David Crosby
Don King
David Cassidy
Dweezil Zappa
Dennis Miller
Donald Trump
Demi Moore
Dr. Joyce Brothers
Dr. Ruth Westheimer
Dr. Stephen Hawking
Debbie Gibson

Diane Parkinson
Denny McClain
Dana Plato
David Carradine
Dan Castellanza

Eartha Kitt
Emo Phillips
Ed Koch
Elton John
Eddie Money
Ed Begley, Jr.
Ed Asner
Easy-E
Ernie Anastos
Edie McClurg

Fabio
Frank Stallone
Flavor Flav
Frank Zappa
Flo and Eddie
Father Guido Sarducci
Fran Drescher
Fred "Rerun" Berry

G. Gordon Liddy
Grandpa Al Lewis
Graham Nash
Gilbert Gottfried
Geraldo Rivera
Gloria Estefan
Garry Shandling
Gene Simmons
Gennifer Flowers
Garry Marshall
George Steinbrenner
George Carlin
Ginger Lynn
Glen Scarpelli

George Wendt

Heidi Fleiss
Howie Mandel
Henny Youngman
Harry Shearer
Hyapatia Lee
Harold Ramis
Heather Locklear

Ian Anderson

James Taylor
Joey Buttafuoco
Joey Ramone
Jim Belushi
Jessica Hahn
Joe Piscipo
Julian Lennon
Judy Tenuta
Jean-Claude Van Damme
Jason Priestly
Jon Bon Jovi
Joe Walsh
Jerry Seinfeld
Jay Leno
Janis Ian
Jack Burce
Joan Rivers
John Stamos
Joe Frazier
Jack Cassidy
Jake LaMotta
John Phillips
Jann Wenner
Jerry Brown
Jamie Lee Curtis
Julie Newmar
Jackie Stallone
James Brown
Joe Clark

Jimmy Breslin
June Foray
Joey Heatherton
John Entwistle
Jimi Hendrix
Joan Jett
Joe Perry

Keith Hernandez
Kevin Kline
Kreskin

Luke Perry
Leslie West
Larry King
Leonard Marshall
Lenny Kravitz
Lou Ferrigno
LaToya Jackson
Linda Blair
Lloyd Lindsay Young
Lorenzo Lamas
Lenny Bruce
Little Richard

Meat Loaf
Mason Reese
Michelle Phillips
Maury Povich
Milton Berle
Mickey Mantle
Morton Downey, Jr.
Marilyn Chambers
Montel Williams
Mary Jo Buttafuoco
Melissa Gilbert
Mario Van Peebles
Moon Unit Zappa
Mickey Dolenz
Mr. Blackwell
Monty Hall

Max Weinberg
Milli Vanilli
Michael McKean
Marilyn Michaels
Mr. T.
Mickey Rooney
Mike Love
May Pang

Nick Rhodes
Noel Redding

Ozzy Osbourne
O.J. Simpson

Patty Smyth
Pee-Wee Herman
Penn Jillette
Pat McCormack
Peter Noone
Peter Max
Paul Schaefer
Pat Cooper
Phoebe Snow
Paul Kantner
Phoebe Cates
Patti Davis
Pete Best
Paco

Rip Torn
Richard Belzer
Richard Simmons
Rodney Dangerfield
Roger Clinton
Richard Pryor
Run-DMC
Roger Daltry
Richard Lewis
Raquel Welch
Rob Lowe

Robin Williams
Robert Englund
Ruth Buzzi
Richie Sambora
Roger McGuinn
Ray Manzarek
Ronnie Spector
Rosie Perez
Robert Blake
Robert Klein
Richard Harris
Robert Vaughn
Rev. Donald Wildmon
Ron Greshner
Richard Marx
Rain Pryor
Rich Little
Reggie Jackson
Robert Cray

Steve Allen
Steven Wright
Sammy Davis, Jr.
Sting
Sam Kinison
Sally Kirkland
Senator Alfonse D'Amato
Siskel and Ebert
Symphony Sid
Sylvester Stallone
Steven Tyler
Slash
Sebastian Bach
Sandra Bernhard
Steve Rossi
Spencer Davis
Steve Garvey
Sally Kellerman
Stevie Ray Vaughan
Shadoe Stevens
Susan Richardson

Stewart Copeland
Steve Guttenberg
Suzanne Vega
Southside Johnny
Steven Baldwin
Sir Mix-a-Lot
Stacey Galina

Tula
Tommy Chong
Tori Spelling
Tawny Kitaen
The Olsen Twins
Tiny Tim
Tom Jones
Timothy Leary
Ted Nugent
Tony Bennett
Tone Loc
Tina Yothers
The Barbie Twins
Tim Conway
The BeeGees
The Cowsills
The Bangles
The Fabulous Thunderbirds
Todd Bridges
T. Bone

Vince Neil

Whoopi Goldberg
Weird Al Yankowitz
Willie Nelson
Wendy O'Williams

Young M.C.

Zsa Zsa Gabor
Zak Starkey

ANSWERS

1. Ted Kennedy
2. (F) Tom Chiusano purchased a state-of-the-art phone system
3. **Russell**
4. "Psychedelic Bee" or "Silver Nickels and Golden Dimes"
5. **Electric Comic Book, Howard Stern's teenage band**
6. (D) **The Chevy Chase Show**
7. Earth Dog Fred, Frightening Fred Norris, or Fred Norris: King of Mars
8. The Howard Stern Phone Line
9. (C) **Testicle Tuck**
10. Jackie Martling
11. (E) **Bob and Ray**
12. Lynn Armandt
13. **Boobshenga**
14. (H) **Incontinent Dial-a-Date**
15. (KK) All of the above.
16. Matthew Broderick, after he was involved in an automobile accident in Europe
17. Bob and Ray
18. Caldor
19. **Sam Kinison**
20. **Luke Perry**
21. Imus
22. (B) June 3, 1987
23. **Reverend Al Sharpton**
24. **$12,000.00**
25. Jerry Seinfeld

26. Soupy Sales

27. # Club Bené, New Jersey

28. Ⓔ WRNW

29. Ⓐ WWDC

30. Ⓓ WCCC

31. Ⓑ WNBC

32. Ⓑ and Ⓕ. He started with Stern at WNBC, but joined the show full-time at WXRK.

33. Ⓕ **WXRK**

34. # Anal Fissures

35. Ⓔ 100 to 124 times, 101 times to be exact

36. **Dee Snider**

37. Ⓓ Camp Wel-Met

38. Bill Boggs

39.

	8	

40. **Lyle Lovett**

41. *Nightlife* with David Brenner

42. # Guitar legend Leslie West

43. Fox TV

44. Ⓒ Petey Green

45. Jackie "Penthouse Platinum Jokepage" Martling

46. # A pontiff

47. # The Flying Nun

48. The F Emmy (F.M.)

49. True *and* False. It's supposed to end at 10 a.m., but it never does.

50. # True

51. True

52. # False. Robin was a nurse, but not in the navy.

53. True

54. **True**

55. **False. Steve O beat Jackie on *Star Search*; however, Jackie did stick his finger up Tony O's butt at a Super Bowl party.**

56. False, Fred Norris was born near Olympus Mons, Mars

57. False. Breast reduction.

58. True. Also Howie, Howch, and Howchala

59. **Siobhan**

60. **Darren the Foot Licker**

61. Crazy Jerry

62. 'Gina Girl

63. **Froggy**

64. **Rachel the Spanker**

65. Fred the Elephant Boy as the Ghost of Speech Impediment Future, Quentin the Stutterer as the Stuttering Scrooge, and the girl that faked Tourette's syndrome, Tammy Tourette.

66. Omer

67. **Celeste**

68. Celestine

69. Ⓔ **Boobshenga**

70. Ⓑ Jerry Nachman

71. **Roosevelt**

72. Howard moved to Rockville Centre.

73. **Frightening Fred Norris**

74. The Martlings, Jackie and Nancy

75. **Tom Chiusano, General Manager/WXRK**

76. The King Schmaltz Bagel Hour

214. 'Gina Man

215. **Friggin'**

216. Mark and Brian

217. Marie Antoinette

218. Melrose Larry Green

219. Shades of Blue

220. **The Grease Man**

221. Fred Norris

222. The Prince's Trust Concert (Royal Albert Hall)

223. Each reported Stern to the FCC

224. **"I Gotta Crow"**

225. ©Jessica Hahn

226. January 12th, 1954

227. The Homo Room

228. *Fifty Ways to Rank Your Mother*

229. Right

230. ⒟Marge Simpson

231. *Scattergories*

232. Leonard Marshall

233. **Large Penis Size**

234. The Blonde Frankenstein

235. Fred Norris, guitarist extraordinaire

236. Up guest's skirts

237. "The Tarantella"

238. ⒟Dick Cavett

239. The Elephant Man

240. ⒝El Greco

241. Don Buchwald

242. ⒝Sigue Sigue Sputnik

243. Shoes

244. Glenn Close

245. Becky the Mental Patient

246. ©Mexico

247. Mark Harris

281. **Joey Buttafuoco**
282. Ⓑ 1982
283. Dell'Abate
284. Arsenio Hall
285. *Mad* Magazine
286. Susan Richardson
287. Pat Cooper
288. Rudy Giuliani, but the investigation was quickly dropped.
289. **Ralph Cirilla**
290. Ⓒ Air Force
291. Transcendental meditation
292. Ⓒ October 24, 1993
293. Richard Belzer
294. Mick Jagger
295. **Angela Bowie**
296. Dr. Stephen Hawking
297. Jimi Hendrix
298. Lenny Bruce
299. Rev. Donald Wildmon
300. **Symphony Sid**

This book is a biographical sketch of the *Howard Stern Show*, from its infancy in college radio to its current status as an icon of contemporary American broadcasting.

The Federal Communications Commission (FCC) has fined the *Howard Stern Show* and Infinity Broadcasting over one million dollars for broadcasting material it deems "patently offensive by contemporary community standards."

How can the *Howard Stern Show* be considered "patently offensive by contemporary community standards" when that "community" chooses to listen to and is directly responsible for making the broadcast achieve its number-one status in recent rating surveys (New York, Philadelphia, and Los Angeles).

The *Howard Stern Show's* growing success in a dozen more markets further illustrates its acceptability by these same "contemporary community standards."

Express your concerns regarding "targeted" censorship in radio free America. Write your congressional representatives and the FCC in support of First Amendment rights and the *Howard Stern Show*.

Sincere thanks to Denise for her photo research, editing, and drive; to Eleanor S. for her determination; to Roger Gorman for the great design; to Andréa Rose for her understanding and support; to Tony Gangi for pulling all this together; and to Len B. for his meticulously documented assistance.

Finally, much respect and special thanks for . . . Great Radio Art.

Ray D. O'Fan

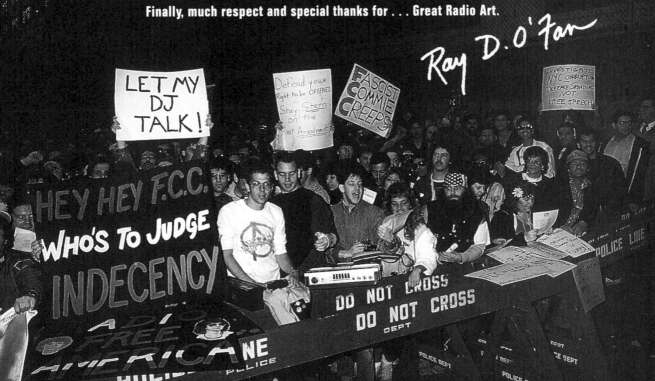

Photo Credits